Live Music!

The Voice

Elizabeth Sharma

Wayland

Titles in the series

Brass	Strings
Keyboards	The Voice
Percussion	Woodwind

TOPIC CHART	MUSIC		Science	Maths	English	Geography	History	Technology	Religious education
	Performing and composing (AT 1)	Listening and appraising (AT 2)							
Chapter 1 Music for everyone	✓	✓	✓		✓	✓			✓
Chapter 2 Songs for the people	✓	✓			✓	✓		✓	
Chapter 3 Voices from long ago		✓			✓	✓	✓		✓
Chapter 4 Don't play around – sing a round	✓	✓		✓	✓				

First published in 1993 by
Wayland (Publishers) Ltd
61 Western Road, Hove
East Sussex BN3 1JD, England

Editor: Cath Senker
Designer: Malcolm Walker
Consultant: Valerie Davies, Primary Adviser,
East Sussex County Council Music School

British Library Cataloguing in Publication Data
Sharma, Elizabeth
  The Voice. – (Live music! series)
  I. Title II. Series
  782

ISBN 0 7502 0451 6

Typeset by Kudos Editorial and Design Services, Sussex, England
Cover artwork by Malcolm Walker
Printed and bound by Casterman S.A., Belgium

Contents

Words printed in **bold** are explained in the glossary.

Music for everyone

Do you sometimes shout, or sometimes whisper? Can you say a rhyme? Or make up a **rhythmic** rap? Can you hum a tune or sing a song?

Your voice is a very special musical instrument. You often use your voice to speak, and sometimes you use it for singing. No one else has a voice exactly the same as yours.

These Welsh children are singing in their school choir. Singing is a very important tradition in Wales. The country is sometimes called the 'land of song'.

When you speak, your voice makes a kind of music, because your words have rhythm. Try saying your name and then clapping the rhythm the words make. Do you ever chant the name of your favourite sports team?

Try humming low, middle and high sounds. Can you feel which part of your body **vibrates** with each sound you make?

(Above) Here is Cleveland Watkiss, a British soul singer of the 1990s.

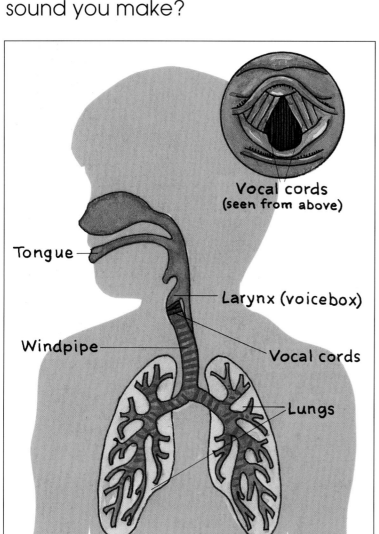

Vocal cords
(seen from above)

Tongue

Larynx (voicebox)

Windpipe

Vocal cords

Lungs

Your voice produces sound in the same way as a musical instrument. The mouth, nose and head act as a sound box, and the lungs push a column of air up the windpipe. This causes the two vocal cords, which are stretched across the larynx, to vibrate and make a sound.

Singing is in the air

Have you ever run out of breath in the middle of a line of song? If you are nervous or excited, you might run out of breath when you are talking, especially if you are trying to say something quickly.

Singers have to practise controlling their breathing to make sure that their voice sounds right, whether they are singing fast or slow, high or low, loud or soft.

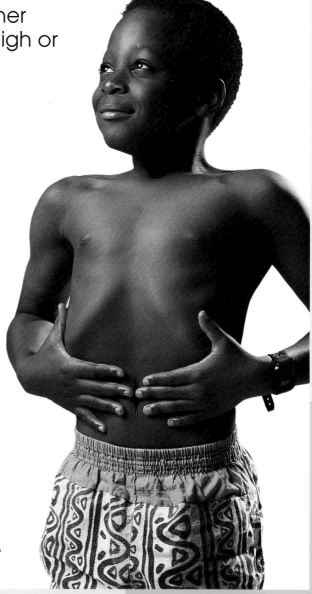

This boy is feeling his lungs fill with air as he breathes in.

When you breathe in, your lungs fill with air, like two balloons. You can feel this. Breathe out slowly until your lungs feel empty. Put your hands on your lower ribs, with your middle fingers just touching. Now breathe in as much air as you can. What happens to your fingers?

You can learn to control your breathing. Try these exercises.
1. Take a deep breath and fill your lungs with air. Purse your lips as if you are going to whistle – but don't whistle! Blow out all the air very slowly.

Count how many seconds you can make your breath last.

2. Take a deep breath and slowly let out the air by singing 'oo' very softly on one note.

3. Take a deep breath, and let out the air by singing 'ah' as loudly as you can without shouting.

What makes you run out of breath more quickly – singing softly or singing loudly?

Singers have to learn to breathe in quickly, and breathe out slowly. They have to decide when to take a breath to fit in with the meaning of the words they are singing, and the shape of the musical **phrases**.

These children are practising their singing. They are trying to make their breath last a long time.

Why do we sing?

This Jewish family in Israel is celebrating the Passover festival. They sing religious songs before eating a special meal.

Think of all the times when we sing. We sing to celebrate birthdays and religious festivals. Most religions of the world have their own songs. They make the ceremonies special, and help people to think about their God.

We often sing when we are happy, and sometimes when we are sad. **Blues** music sounds sad. People sing of their troubles in a blues song.

Singing together makes people feel as though they belong. Most peoples of the world have their own songs. The songs tell stories about their history and help to keep traditions alive.

People often sing when they are angry about something. These South Africans are singing in protest against the government.

Each sports team has supporters who like to sing their own songs. Often they are well-known songs, with the words changed.

It is much easier to learn something if it is made into a song. Babies and small children learn from nursery rhymes and counting songs. You could make up a song to help children to remember spelling rules.

This little boy is learning a counting song with his mother.

Arrange a range

Try singing the lowest note you possibly can. Now sing your highest note. Find these notes on the piano. The notes that you can comfortably sing make up your singing **range**. See if your friends have a higher or a lower range than you.

This girl sings high notes. The man sings lower notes.

Basses are men who sing the lowest notes.

Baritones sing in between tenors and basses.

Tenors are men who sing high notes.

Contraltos are women who sing lower than altos.

Altos are women who sing low notes.

Mezzo sopranos sing in between sopranos and altos.

Sopranos are women who sing high notes.

Ask a male teacher to sing his highest and lowest notes, and find them on the piano. If a man and a woman sing the same tune, the man's voice will usually sound an **octave** lower. He has a lower range than the woman. Children have a high range, like many women. Sing with a male teacher and listen to the difference in your voices.

This picture shows a choir with all the voice parts.

In music for choirs, there are tunes at different **pitches** to suit the high voices and the low voices. The tunes fit together in **harmony** with each other. The **composer** wrote them so that they would sound good together.

Songs for the people

All over the world people sing songs about their everyday lives, and the things that make them happy or sad. These are called folk songs.

Folk songs are often made up by people who are not trained musicians. The **melodies** are usually simple, and fun to sing. They are easy for people who speak the same language to remember. Folk music is usually passed on from one singer to another. In most parts of the world, it is not written down.

Much folk music around the world is based on a five-note **scale** called the **pentatonic scale**. This scale is easy to sing. You can play pentatonic tunes on a musical instrument, using the notes C,D,E,G and A. Maybe you know the Scottish tune *Ye Banks and Braes*, or *Amazing Grace*. Both use the pentatonic scale.

These are folk musicians in the Channel Islands. The guitar, violin, accordion and penny whistle are often played in folk music.

Many Chinese melodies are in the pentatonic scale, and so are lots of Indian melodies.

It is quite easy to compose good tunes using the pentatonic scale. First of all, write the words for your song. Then make up a melody on the piano or xylophone. If you can sing it to your friends, and they can sing it back to you, you have composed a good folk tune.

This is a group of dancers from the Punjab, India, playing bangra music. Bangra is traditional Punjabi folk music. A new kind of bangra has become popular with Indians in Britain. They play electronic instruments, and the singers often rap in Punjabi.

Dance to the music

People all over the world dance to folk songs accompanied by hand clapping, stamping, or simple percussion instruments.

In many parts of Africa, India, the Polynesian Islands and the Maori areas of New Zealand, large groups of people get together to dance and sing rhythmic songs. It can be very exciting to watch.

In the Highlands of Scotland, people make 'mouth music'. They sing short rhythmic phrases, which are repeated over and over again.

These people in Western Samoa, in the Pacific Ocean, are singing and moving together in a large group.

The words do not make much sense, but they are sung for their rhythmic sound. People dance to this music.

In Arab and African countries, it is quite usual for a leading singer to sing a phrase, which is repeated, or answered, by the other singers. This is called a 'call and response' song. Many of these songs accompany dances. Gospel music follows this style. People sing, clap and perform simple dance steps as part of a Christian religious ceremony.

Gospel singers use music when they praise God. These American women are clapping while they sing a hymn in church.

Live Music!

Long ago, people realized that singing made the human voice sound more magical, and gave special meaning to words.

The early Jews and Christians used to sing parts of their religious books out loud. The Catholic church developed very strict rules about which melodies could be used. At the end of the sixth century AD, Pope Gregory I collected these melodies. They were very simple songs, and this music became known as plainsong. Some plainsong is still sung today.

We know from paintings that people in ancient times used to sing. This Roman mosaic from the first century AD shows an actor playing the tambourine. He is probably accompanying singing and dancing.

This manuscript from the fifteenth century shows monks praying to God. Monks often used to sing their prayers. They wrote down the melodies, and some are still sung in Catholic churches today.

In Europe, only monks were educated enough to write down their melodies. The songs sung by the ordinary people, just for fun, were passed on from person to person.

In the eleventh and twelfth centuries in France, travelling minstrels called troubadours, or *trouvères*, used to visit the courts of the noblemen, singing songs of love, bravery and legends. They accompanied themselves on the lute or lyre.

Madrigals

In Europe in the sixteenth century, all well-educated women and men were expected to be able to play musical instruments and to sing. They often sang songs called madrigals. There were several different melodies in a madrigal, weaving in and out of each other. This music was called polyphonic music, which means 'many sounds'.

Madrigals were first composed in Italy, but they became very popular in England.

This is a musical party in the seventeenth century. The singers are reading their voice parts from music.

Opera – stories in song

Opera is a very exciting kind of play, with singing instead of talking. Musical instruments help to make a big, loud sound in the dramatic parts of the opera.

Opera is popular around the world, especially in China and Japan, and in Europe.

This is a Chinese opera being performed.

Opera in Europe started to develop at the end of the sixteenth century in Italy. A composer called Claudio Monteverdi wrote operas with dramatic stories. He composed **solo** songs, called arias, for the main characters. Musical instruments accompanied the singers.

If you listen to the Italian language being spoken, you will hear the open 'O' sounds and the rhythm of the words. It is a very musical language, perfect for singing in operas.

This picture shows a dramatic scene from the opera Tosca, *by the Italian composer, Puccini.*

Italian operas composed in the nineteenth century became very popular. Verdi and Puccini wrote operas with beautiful melodies and interesting plots. They were loved by the people who went to see them, and are still popular today.

Look in the library for a book of opera stories, and try to find cassettes or CDs of the opera music.

This is the Italian singer, Luciano Pavarotti. He has helped to make opera music popular among people who have never been to see an opera.

Popular music from Africa

Do you like pop music? Next time you listen to your favourite singer or band, think of the hard lives of the people who formed the beginnings of much of the music you enjoy today.

In the eighteenth and nineteenth centuries, European slave-traders took West Africans away from their homes, against their will. They were forced to work as slaves on cotton and sugar **plantations** in the Caribbean, and in the southern states of America.

This picture from the early twentieth century shows a cotton plantation in Tennessee, USA. The work was very hard. The workers used to sing to cheer themselves up.

This is the American soul singer, Aretha Franklin. Soul music developed in the 1960s in the USA, and became popular again in the early 1990s.

The Africans brought with them their songs, with exciting rhythms. When they were **converted** to Christianity, they added these rhythms to Christian hymns. This is how spirituals developed, and then later, gospel music. In the 1960s, soul music grew from the musical style of gospel, with words about love and romance instead of religion.

Other forms of popular music come from African rhythms. Often, the African workers on the plantations were not allowed to talk during work, but they were allowed to sing. They sang rhythmic songs to help them to work together. Or they made up call and response songs called 'field hollers'.

People sang about their troubles, and this was the beginning of blues music. An accompaniment based on three guitar **chords** was later added, and this led to rhythm and blues music in the 1940s, then rock and roll in the 1950s.

Bob Marley was a very famous reggae singer. He sang about his wish for peace and freedom for all.

The African tradition of chanting stories in a rhythmic way developed in Jamaica, and in Britain, into 'toasting'. DJs would talk over the reggae records they played.

Rap follows the same idea, but the beat is faster and electronic sounds are often used. The rhymes are shouted above a heavy beat, with **bass** and melody **samples** added. Rap words are usually about the difficulties of everyday life, not about love and romance. Can you make up a rap about life at school?

This is the American rap group Public Enemy. Many of their raps are about the hard life of black people in the USA.

Singing is great fun, especially when people sing different melodies at the same time. Everyone needs to listen to one another so that they sing in tune and in time together.

A round is a special kind of song in which different groups sing the same song, but at slightly different times.

Try this round. Divide into two groups. Group 1 starts singing. When the singers have sung four **bars**, group 2 starts singing. When each group reaches the end of the song, the singers start again. Clap while you sing to help you to keep in time together.

Row row row your boat, gently down the stream.

Merrily merrily merrily merrily, life is but a dream.

Now divide into four groups. Group 1
starts singing. After two bars, group 2
starts singing, and so on until all the
groups are singing.

Now try this beautiful Hebrew song.
This time, divide into three groups.
Each group starts eight bars after the
group before. The words mean
'Cause us to return Lord, to you,
and we shall return. Renew our days
of old.'

Ha-shi -ve -nu ha-shi -ve -nu A- do -nai e - le - cha.

Ve - na shu - va, Ve - na shu - va.

Cha - desh Cha - desh ya - meinuke ke - deem.

Two together

It is great fun to sing two different songs at once, but you have to be sure they fit together.

Try this: group 1 sings part 1, a song called *Jamaica Farewell*, and group 2 sings part 2, a song called *Tie Me Kangaroo Down Sport.*

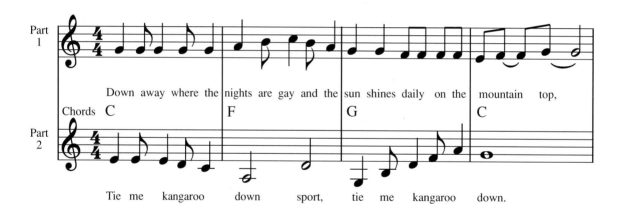

Part 1: Down away where the nights are gay and the sun shines daily on the mountain top,

Chords: C F G C

Part 2: Tie me kangaroo down sport, tie me kangaroo down.

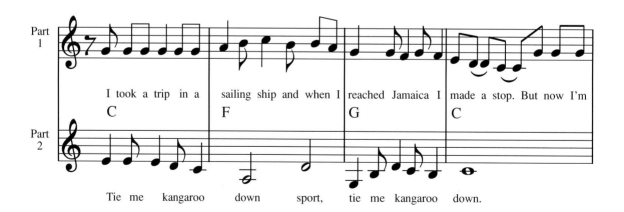

Part 1: I took a trip in a sailing ship and when I reached Jamaica I made a stop. But now I'm

C F G C

Part 2: Tie me kangaroo down sport, tie me kangaroo down.

Each pair of children is singing a different part in a song. First of all, each pair practised their part until they could sing it well.

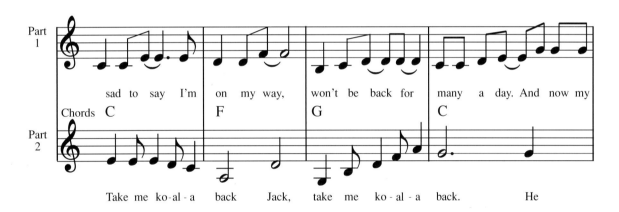

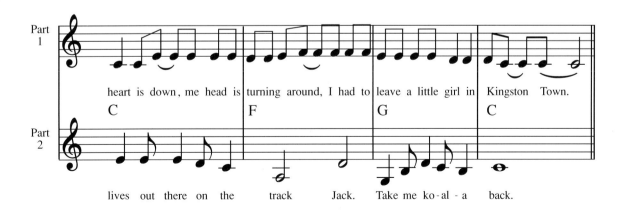

Glossary

Bars   Small sections of written music. Each bar has the same number of beats in it. This is a bar of music.

Bass   The bass is the part in a band which plays the lowest notes. It is often played on an electric guitar or a double-bass.

Blues   Early jazz music that developed from the songs of Africans living in the USA.

Chords   Groups of notes that are played together to make a good sound.

Composer   A person who writes music.

Converted   Changed to another religion.

Harmony   The playing together of two or more tunes to make a pleasing sound.

Melodies   The correct musical term for tunes.

Octave   The eight-note distance between two musical notes of the same name but different pitch.

Pentatonic scale   A scale that is made up of five notes. The most common pentatonic scale consists of C,D,E,G and A.

Phrase   A short part of a melody.

Pitch   How high or low a note sounds.

Plantations   Large fields where crops are grown.

Range   The notes you can comfortably sing, from the lowest to the highest, make up your range.

Rhythmic   Having a regular beat.

Samples   Musical phrases borrowed from other records.

Scale   A group of musical notes going up or down at fixed intervals.

Solo   A part of a piece of music written for just one instrument or singer.

Vibrates   When something shakes very quickly back and forth, it is said to vibrate.

Finding out more

1. Why not listen to some music for the voice?
Here are some ideas:
Folk music: *Chinese Classical Folk Music* by Arc Music.
Gospel music: Songs by Mahalia Jackson and Andrae Crouch.
Madrigals: English madrigals by William Byrd, Thomas Tallis and John Wilbye. Italian madrigals by Giovanni Palestrina.
Opera: *Rigoletto* by Guiseppe Verdi.
The song, *Nessun Dorma*, sung by Luciano Pavarotti. It is from *Turandot* by Giacomo Puccini.
Plainsong: The best-known style is Gregorian chant. You can still hear it sung in some Roman Catholic churches.
Soul music: Singers James Brown, Aretha Franklin, Otis Redding.

2. Watch music programmes on television. There are often concerts and operas, as well as pop programmes. Sometimes, musicals are shown.

3. Try to hear some live music. Ask if you can listen to a rehearsal of a local church choir. Most areas have a youth choir that gives concerts – the tickets will be quite cheap. There might be a folk group you could listen to. Ask at your local library for information.

Useful books

Opera: What's All the Screaming About? by Roger Englander (Walker and Co., USA, 1983)
Folk Music by Clive Griffin (Dryad, 1989)
Pop Cults by Kay Rowley (Wayland, 1991)
Singing Sack: 28 Song-stories from Around the World by Helen East (A&C Black, 1989)
Songs of Protest and Civil Rights by Jerry Silverman (Chelsea House, USA, 1992)
Voice and Music Management by Alyn Shipton (Heinemann, 1991)

Index

Page numbers in **bold** indicate subjects shown in pictures as well as in the text.

Acknowledgements

The photographs in this book were provided by: Clive Barda 20; Camera Press (H Benson) 15; Compix (D Cole) 14; David Cumming 15; ET Archives 16, 17, 18; Eye Ubiquitous (J Waterlow) 19; Impact 4 (S Benbow); Life File 5 (J Hoare), (N Sutton) 9 (below), (M Maidment) 12; Link (O Eliason) 9 (above); Photri 8; Popperfoto 22; Redferns (N Sansar) 13; Rex Features 21, 23, 24, 25; Wayland Picture Library (A Blackburn) 6, (Z Mukhida) *cover* and 29, (I Lilly) 7. Artwork: Tony de Saulles 5, 10, 11.
The publishers would like to thank the staff and pupils of Hove Park School, East Sussex, for their kind co-operation.